Hummingbirds

Vol. 2

Poetry and Art

by

Mallory Eaglewood

English version of Oiseau-Mouches, also written by
Mallory Eaglewood

Copyrights © 2023 par Mallory Eaglewood

www.malloryeaglewood.com

Art by Mallory Eaglewood

Text by Mallory Eaglewood

All rights reserved. No part of this publication may be reproduced in any form or by any means, electronic or mechanical, including photocopying, recording or any information browsing, storage or retrieval system, without written permission from Mallory Eaglewood.

ISBN :

Distributed commercially by The Ingram Book Company.

Other books by Mallory Eaglewood:

- Throwaway People – A novel about the historic suffering of Residential Schools for Canada's Indigenous children and the generational trauma it caused.
- The Good Life – Humourous short stories about sailing on a small boat in the South Pacific Ocean in the 1970s.
- Pink Pistachios – A novel and play about how one person's psychological crisis alters the lives of three friends during the exciting and changing musical and literary period of the 1970s in Vancouver, Canada.
- Oiseaux-mouches – The French poetry, in this little book, explores the complexity of human love.
- Hummingbirds Vol 1. - Poems that will make you laugh, bring tears of joy or sobs of sadness. Disconcerted, titillated or angry, you will reflect and be moved.

CONTENTS

DEDICATION	i
ACKNOWLEDGMENTS	ii
ABOUT THE AUTHOR	iii
SHIPS PASSING	1
EVENING BY THE LAKE	3
THE MAN UNDER THE RASPBERRY UMBRELLA	5
A L I V E	7
Not Here	10
BECAUSE YOU'RE THERE	13
ONCE UPON A TIME	16
LOVE	19
THE SINGER	21
LOVE IN THE DARK	24
ARCTIC ARCADIA	28
THIS IS LIFE	30
I'LL WALTZ YOU TO THE MOON	31
I'D LIKE YOU TO MEET…	34
WHEN PASSION RULED	38
. . . PLAY ON	40

THE REFRAIN OF A SHOWER 43

THOUGHTS 46

SPEAKING 47

COMIN' THRO THE RYE 48

THE INFINITE WALTZ 51

MADRIGAL OF FIRE 53

TOGETHER 55

SUNSHINE 56

END OF AN AFFAIRE 57

GLOOM INTO BRIGHTNESS 59

THE PRIZE 63

MUSIC OF COMMUNION 65

THE BELLS OF SURRENDER 66

WHERE SELF-WORTH IS 68

AFTER CREMATION 71

AFTER THE STORM 73

ENDURING 75

OPENING THE GATE 76

PASO DOBLE 78

DEDICATION

Whatever merit I have gained through this effort, I dedicate to all living beings.

ACKNOWLEDGMENTS

With respect and gratitude, I acknowledge the privilege of living and working on SD̲ÁY̲ES (Pender Island), part of the unceded, ancestral lands of the WSÁNEĆ people. I am mindful of the cultural impacts of ongoing colonialism and dispossession of all Indigenous peoples throughout the world.

ABOUT THE AUTHOR

Eaglewood has lived and worked in Canada, Scotland, England, Germany and Greece. She has had a career in education, working as a department head, lecturer and course programmer in English literature.

Additionally, her fascinating life includes experiences as an officer in the Canadian army, a meditation mentor in a Buddhist abbey, and PA to a CEO of a $200 million engineering project in India.

She's faced a shooter in the Syrian desert at midnight, and a few sharks ten meters below the surface while scuba diving off the coast of Bali.

A decorated author, Mallory has received the prestigious title of Author of the Year from the provincial newspaper, and her articles can be found in various journals. Her previous books include poetry, short stories and plays in English. As a member of the Federation of BC Writers and the League of Canadian Poets, she is an active presence in the literary community.

SHIPS PASSING

Dancing with the man I never had:
Did your eyes see some past love,
 when you looked at me?
Did your arms feel Her
 when you held me close?
Did you hear Her tender voice
 when I whispered in your ear?

 I never called you mine.
 We stood so close but
 You were too far away.
 My one true love
 That still grips my heart.

Dancing with the woman I never had:
Why did your eyes turn away
 when, finally I saw you?
Why didn't my embrace comfort you,
 when it took so long to hold you?
Why did my words not reach you,
  when all past girls disappeared with your coming?

 You never called me yours.
 We stood so close but
 you were so far away.
 My one true love
 That still grips my heart.

Dancing with the man I never had:
    Did you miss Her so much?
    I could have loved you more.
Each step in our dance
    Could have lasted forever.

    Should I have called you mine?
    Should I have shouted out my love?
    My one true love
    That still grips my heart.

Dancing with the woman I never had:
    Was there nothing I could have done?
    Did I leave too many words unspoken?
When we danced, I was in heaven.
    It could have lasted forever.

    Should I have called you mine?
    Should I have shouted out my love?
    My one true love
    That still grips my heart.

Dancing with the beloved I never had:
    I drift alone dreaming of you.
    I drift alone wondering why.
A chance not snatched and never returned.
    I drift alone, still in love with you.

EVENING BY THE LAKE

I am in the chair on the right.
Throughout the warm afternoon,
I read. Beside the empty chair on my left.

Now, as the sun begins to set
and the gentle evening zephyrs
waft in from the lake. I drift.

Gardenia and Night Blooming Jasmine,
attracting their pollinators,
Intoxicate me.

The memory of
those feelings
begin to come back.

I'll be there late in the long night
listen to the Whip-poor-will
calling for love.

And then I will meditate
in the dark,
reluctant to break the spell.

Of want no longer is.

THE MAN UNDER
THE RASPBERRY UMBRELLA

One day while walking down Le Grand Avenue,
Sitting in a terraced café under a raspberry umbrella,
A man sat drinking his early morning coffee,
A small biscuit on a plate near his arm.

A feral lock of chestnut hair, hung evocatively
Above his dark, dark eyes, staring at nothing at all.
I continued on my way, but the man came with me -
I could not shake his handsome image from my mind.

Did those eyes express a despondent heart?
Had his lover forsaken him? Or did she die tragically,
one summer's day, leaving an empty heart
in this man, sitting alone in the Grand Café?

I grieve for you, man I've never met. I share your pain
On this glorious day with the all the Maple trees
raising their arms to the sky in gladness, while
lonely people walk aimlessly, or sit unaccompanied.

I imagine you are tall, man whose name I do not know.
Perhaps you are called Oliver, my friend from the café.
I wonder. what it would be like to drink coffee with you,
sitting under the raspberry umbrellas.

I think of us dancing, with me swinging in your arms,
Under the stars, where only we two waltz in warm
Breezes, and talk of tomorrows and kiss passionately
Before leaving the world behind closed curtains.

Would we greet every morning, wrapped tenderly
In each other's arms? Would you whisper your love
Into my ear? Your desire enchants me, my man,
There are things I wait for you to teach me.

I turn, run back to the café of the raspberry umbrellas.
I rush to your arms. I want to kiss away your sorrow.
What is in our stars, I long to explore, beloved.
I arrive for my destiny.

But the chair is already vacant.

ALIVE

*You shone your light
on my solitary, still soul
and surprised
my heart into a tango afresh*

    *and in an instant
    my breath,
        long solemn and dulled,
            leaped back into life.*

*The song in your breast instantly
became our duet*

*Your brightness reached into the depths
                        of my soul
Clasped both my hands and steered me
                        so softly
Between the night stars
in the endless dark sky.*

*And a dream I'd tucked
willingly
into my past
    took flight.*

*I read a soft message in your hungry brown eyes
Galaxies of treasures rushed into my mind and
just when I had felt it could never again happen
truths came to burn onto my so matured skin.*

You twinkled your blessings
  in my jaded awareness
Showed me new joy
  in a morning's glad glow

Yes, you gave me a sweet love
  But your dark eyes did not offer
Continuance into red setting suns.
  All that was there was the now.

Only for now.

Tomorrow will hold your sweet body
  in damp earth.
For deep in your bones grows
a rival too strong.
She has you and will take you.

There's nothing I can do.

But I have a thing
      far greater than bones
           that the earth cannot share.

Your warmth
      And your comfort
         will stay in my soul.
              A sharing to last far longer
      than breath.

I rejoice in our coupling
Rejoice in a new me,
      I even rejoice in the future

For the memoirs of
         our walks in the forests,
         swimming in the sea,
         sweet whispers of greetings,
         and your kisses
are my comfort in your absence.

Because now,
    I can look forward
       to continuing alone.

Bring on the future!

For the light that you shone
no matter how brief
    will brightened
        my soul
            to the end of my days.

NOT HERE

I think of you.
So far away.
Before sleeping,
And on waking.

I recall so vividly:
Lying beside you at night,
And in our waking hours,
Sharing eggs and toast.

I feel aloneness,
Acute and deep.
There is a hunger in me
that spells both pain and joy.

My lips miss the pressure
of your lips! My skin misses
the wetness of your sweat
that you leave on my skin!

In my mind, I breath
into your thick hair,
as you rest your head
On my chest and I feel complete.

My mind holds your scent
That is only you!
My hand feels your strong hand,
So far away now!

You have a softness,
Beneath your strength!
That fills me, and enchants me,
With a deep desire for more.

*The longer you are away,
the more I ache for you,
I lie here alone
wanting and waiting.*

*Feel me beside you when you sleep,
My arms holding you in the night,
Feel my breath in your hair
Our skin sharing each other.*

*I send you strength
to do your work,
To finish quickly
So you can return.*

*When you are done,
Follow your heart home
To us who wait. There are
a thousand kisses yet undelivered.*

BECAUSE YOU'RE THERE

"Because you're there."
I asked you why you love me
It startled me, your words.
I felt an angry nibble rise.

"Because you're there."
You said to me, a day when
The sun was blessing the world.
A tear threatened to surface.

"Because you're there.
When I come home after a brief parting
You want to be in my arms, and
Me in yours. I know this, beloved.

"Because you're there.
When I fight the good fight, and lose,
When I fight the good fight and win.
You want to hear, understand, share.

"Because you're there.
I don't have to struggle to be heard,
I don't have to struggle to be so precise
I don't have to struggle to find common ground.

"Because you're there.
I don't have to seek new love
With all its terror and uncertainty
And worry and self-doubt.

"Because you're there
We have a will to come to terms
A will to work things out
A will to be with me

"Because you're there.
You show me in a thousand ways that
You want me, need me, hunger for me
That my exploring, need, hunger is welcome

"Because you're there
I laugh more than I used to.
I have courage I never knew I had.
I believe I can climb that mountain now.

"Because you're there.
There, standing solidly on your own two feet.
You are with me by choice, not addiction.
As a lover and a friend, I chose you.

*"Because you are there,
No matter how far I am away,
Or how long we must be apart
I'm not alone.*

*"Because you are there
Friendships can fall, hockey teams lose,
Rains come, disappointments assault me.
You're there and my world will survive.*

*"Because you are there
Whether I am near or far
I detect a 'something' in you
I want to cling to.*

*"I love you
Because you are there."*

ONCE UPON A TIME

The sun is not yet touching the far horizon,
Yet the sea sends it's sparkles to my eyes.
There is a breeze kissing my cheek as I rock.
They've all gone home now, to their busy lives.
And I sit on our verandah and my heart smiles.

It is the first August that the father of my children's
Chair is empty. The creak of his rocker is silent
As I sit remembring the laughter and the songs,
At our family's summer haven on Big Trout Lake.
So many Augusts, so many sunsets, so many parties.

Generations played by the lake and more will come.
Though soon my journeys to this gentle shore
Will be ended too. My next great adventure is near.
So I reflect, and sigh, and smile; not tired, not wakeful
Letting the memories drift in and out like butterflies.

This evening on the verandah, I listen to the gentle
Sound of waves, enjoying the stillness.
Not of my husband, or of our sons,.
My memories alight on a time very long ago.
In another time, another place, and other people.

Was his name Robert? Only the name has faded.
His head was the colour of autumn wheat.
The tunes on the breeze, so gentle, they sang to us.
The scent of the pair-blossoms anxious to be fruitful.
We sat in the tall spikey grass, watching the sun's decent.

That boy and I, by chance encounter, two hours in splendor.
I feel the moisture on his hand that held mine so softly.
I smell the scent of his cheek that rested upon mine,
Endless tomorrows spoke to me from his dark young eyes.

once upon a time.

LOVE

When your arms
  are around me
    I feel like
Home

You give me
  breath
    and I'm
Alive

My little self
  Expands
    To be
The universe of love

My Ego
  Is replaced
    By the
Us.

THE SINGER

LOVE IN A GRACEFUL NOTE

*Sing to me of love
On early morning dew.
Sing gently into my heart
With your tender melodies.*

*Tango me to love
In dusk's calm warmth,
And pour into my ears
Your sweet love 'til dawn*

*Waltz me to love,
I'll respond with joy
I'll meet you there
on the edge of the moon*

*Whisper me to love
Among the hidden spaces
Between the light and dark
Beyond the distant stars*

*Breath to me of love
Where we can dance
Till the sun returns
Among the sighing trees.*

*I hear you at midnight
Loving me so gently,
Or devouring my soul
With unbridled passion.*

*Your strong and low octaves
Make my bones tremble,
And your notes so high
Ignite my heart.*

*Because love is like a dream
And you are the opiate.
Singing across the continents
Exploding my senses.*

*For we can own the galaxy
And surrender to love.
Until you are spent
Upon your stage.*

LOVE IN THE DARK

The sun has long left the skies.
The night has wrapped its arms around me.
It strokes me and rocks me.
In the darkness.

Soft rain calls my mind to the forest
Where we picked wild blueberries
Last July, and the grosbeaks eyed at us
And the chickadees scolded us.

Outside the window, the sea taps the shore,
Tickles the empty shells and driftwood
where we lost the world strolling last spring
in the chilled waters and blazing sunshine.

The smell of the earth from across the sea,
floats on the night air and crickets chatter.
They tease my nose and my ears.
The room vibrates with echoes of our tenderness.

*And the words, those words,
now engraved
in the walls,
Can still be heard.*

*Moon beams through the skylight
Reveal more than I need, more than I want.
Come sleep. Take me sleep.
But sleep does not obey.*

Remembered touch warms my skin,
I feel you call me close.
But our words are silent this night.
I don't lean towards you, not tonight.

Oh, that those words would again,
Shout to the stars. That the pull
And response shake the night
And together we could dance.

I reach out to the table by our bed
and take your letter once more.
Next to my chest: no need to reread.
It is written in my bones.

Its shape, its smell, its texture.
Its pages give me comfort.
Breathing into it
As if to give it life

"My Dear, my desire touches my whole,
As you will, when finally, I open our door again
And feel you in my arms, solid and enduring,
Your breath against my face.

"My Dear, my long days are softened
Only by the thought of you.
Missing you is a sweet pain
Strengthened as each day goes by.

"My Dear, the longing marks my heart,
My mind, my hands, my arms.
Every inch of me suffers from
Our separation.

"My Dear, are you yearning for me too?
Do you recall our togetherness?
Do you cherish my touch
when I caress your cheek?"

My Beloved, I come to you in
Moments of quiet.
Hear me – you know how I feel
Open your arms, I will fill them.

My Beloved, I come to you in
Hour of your waking,
And when you lie down at night.
I'm there with you beloved.

"Soon I will be coming.
To the home that is you.
For where you are,
I dwell."

ARCTIC ARCADIA

*We raced, with joy in our hearts,
across the snowy tundra.*

*The moon lighting our speedy way.
Cassiopeia hard pressed to keep up
Or blinded by the sun on a summer's day.*

*The Thelon River's Arctic Char,
In chilled flowing waters
We hunted, together, in spring.*

*We watched Cariboo migrating
And muskox and sometimes owls
So close on our long distant journeys.*

*In spring's Purple Saxifrage, or in caves
Deep under Rock cliffs, my beloved and I,
Lay down together, in our joy.*

*Long before Inuit, long before the Dorset,
long before spears and guns and boats,
Together we traced the valleys and hills.*

*With our throats held high, we thanked the moon
When, full splendored and silvered,
We sang of our love with a melody so sweet.*

*Generations we birthed, each nurtured
With care, who gave our love immortality,
In the land of the midnight sun.*

*We lived our lives together 'til our time ran out.
First my man left me alone in the snow,
I cried to the moon, the melody no longer sweet.*

And not able to breathe without my beloved,
He returned to me so gentle one dark night,
Put feathers in my hair and led me up to the stars.

If you look between the green dancing lights,
You can see us still together on a winter's night,
Looking down on the land, where we once dwelled.

Where we once raced, with joy in our hearts,
 across the snowy tundra.

THIS IS LIFE

Abandon yourself to love
To life
To joy
To good times

Without regret
Without reservation

Especially
Without hesitation

I'LL WALTZ YOU TO THE MOON
(Singer–song writer Eroça Dancer composed a song for this poem.)

'I'll waltz you to the moon tomorrow night,
When we are finally together again.
I will drink the warmth of your touch
And savour the smell of your skin.

Our cheeks will caress while the moon bathes us
Our hunger will consume the absence we share.
I will explore the crevasses of your divine body
And breathe in your tenderness beneath me."

These words you spoke over the phone that day.
I heard your desire and felt your warmth in my ear.
So softly you sang of that coupling, we waited for.
Drifting between heaven and light, soon to be engulfing us.

How long ago, was that tender declaration?
How its remembrance remains so clear and close.
Does it box me, enclose me, steal me away
From living in this world that goes on in ignorance.

I stumble through a life, that is neither present or tangible,
Walking the familiar strange streets,
Hearing accustomed voices that pass without recognition.
In my trance, which clings to me so cruelly indifferent.

Your strides toward our coupling, I can feel in the earth
Day after day. On and on, month after year, in my fog.
Can you see me here? Can you feel my heart?
In my singular world?

'I'll waltz you to the moon tomorrow night,
When we are finally together again.
I will drink the warmth of your touch
And savour the smell of your skin.

Our cheeks will caress while the moon bathes us
Our hunger will consume the absence we share.
I will explore the crevasses of your divine body
And breathe in your tenderness beneath me."

   I'm listening, but the footfalls ended
  A long time ago, a close distance from here,
  In a train, by a cliff,
          descending into a cherished hateful Sea.

    That thief that stole my life.

I'D LIKE YOU TO MEET...

I lived so long in the dark
      Not knowing   myself
           The imagine in the mirror
         Not the one I wanted

I have walked so long
      Ignoring that friend
         Always unappreciated
         But constantly there

I turned my back
      On the one who was always
         So loyal and caring
         And took the lone road

Support, you so kindly offered
      in times of stress   I rejected
         So faced my troubles, regrets
         Loves and losses   all alone

Years went by, without accepting your hand
      To hold me in quiet affection
         In the night, in the sun
         In my sorrow and pain

'No' didn't stop you and
    though deafness didn't lessen with trying
        Rejection didn't break heart
        despite my abuse

Thoughts often repeated:

"Who are
you kidding"
"You're aren't
likeable"
"You'll
embarrass me"

Remember in grade 8, I'd say:

"Your hips are
too big"
"You're no good
at math"
"Your nose is all
wrong"

At that dancing school fall:

"You're so
clumsy"
"You'll never be a
dancer"
"Everybody else is so
much better"

Why did I never notice
  my most special companion?

How could I have given you
  all the abuse?

What kind of a friend
  Would put up with it?

Why have you stayed"
Why do you still love me?

                              "I'm sorry,
                                   Self,
                              so sorry."

                              "That I never
                                loved you
                                 better."

Why did I waste all this time
when we could've been
such good friends?

                              And shared it all.

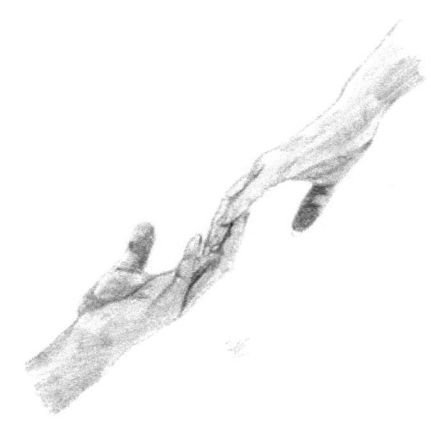

So, SELF,

    Before it is too late,
    Listen to me..
    I'd be delighted to get to know

        Me.

      Beautiful

        Me.

WHEN PASSION RULED

Rain.
An afternoon.
A busy street.

Busy people hurrying by. Did anyone notice?
A couple.
Under an umbrella.
Kissing.
.

Time under command of passion.
Would they have noticed?
I stopped. Noticed. Understood.

When two could bend time and space.
Communicating. Lips against lips?
Attentive. Engrossed. Involved.

Gone now.
Into the mist.
Those days left only in
Remembering.
Long ago.

Attentive. Engrossed. Involved.
Communicating. Lips on lips?
When we could bend time and space.

If one stopped. Would they understand?
Would we have noticed?
Time under command of passion.

A couple.
Under an umbrella.
Kissing.
Busy people hurrying by. Did we notice?

A busy street.
An afternoon.
Rain.

... PLAY ON
(Music is the food of love)

*A fire crackles
In the late evening,
Creating a dance between
Light and dark.*

*A flute wafts soft breezes
To surrendering violins.
Chimes gently guide
A bass drum's rumble.*

*A voice,
Determined, restrained
Like a waterfall
Earnest, imperative.*

*Reflections swaying,
Exterior disintegrating.
Slowly, completely,
Heart-ship follows.*

*Heart's rhythm? – or drums.
Sound and body fuse,
I envision the dance,
I become the dance.*

*Physical laws
No longer apply.
To soft melodies,
I can but surrender*

*With the singer, I waltz
to Saturn, or Mars,
Leaving companions
Imaginary, or real.*

*A voice ripe and young,
Enunciating each tone,
The sound conveying sense,
words superfluous.*

*A pulse connecting sound,
Bone, flesh, emotions, desires,
In the present moment.
Concordance.*

*Movement no longer controllable;
My body governed by the music
With linguistic sensuality,
My body sings the words.*

*Urgency to communicate,
Insisted from deep inside,
Uses harshness of desire,
To escape body.*

Intangible laws
No longer apply.
Sensuality's skin
announces "I'm alive!"

Cherished, longed-for agony,
Each emotion expressed
His voice quavers
And ensnares.

Fully abandoned
Rushing to meet
On-coming desire,
Beyond balance.

Delicious pain
vital yet numbing
Floating pleasure
The stream has no long an end.

Making love all along
This lover of Infinite form,
I am the succubus
I come for me.

My soul reaching out,
The barrier broken
allowing truths to surface
from the great ocean within.

THE REFRAIN OF A SHOWER

*Splashing on my skin,
coming from above,
your voice left a tattoo in its passing,*

*Warm spray envelops like a cloud,
secure, safe.
Touching, tempting, tickling,*

*Banishing alienism from my pores,
seeing the world
newly cleaned; a whole different realm.*

*Cascades of water are words speaking to my heart.
Written on my flesh,
the word I ache for is desire*

*Liquid mingling through my hair, into eyes,
falling from my lips,
Leaving my ears, to stroke my neck.*

*Like rivulets over my breasts,
haunting places forgotten,
The fruit of words, naming un-nameable pleasure.*

*Following every curve,
unstoppable in its journey
Exploring a sense, engraving a memory*

*Evocative. A slender column of heat,
Sending vitality through veins.
Animating the mist. Solidifying you in my mind.*

*Remembering your impact, like a wind from the east,
unbidden, rushing across a desert.
To me, to me. You came.*

*Into the small of my back, your hand, tenderly paused.
Remembering your teasing
lifts me to higher planes.*

*Leaving your mark on my skin forever by the notes
you sang. A burning. A sweet pain.
Forever burnished into my mind.*

*A caress leaving want. You know. You always knew.
A sunbeam offering desire.
You gave. Always you'll give.*

*Trinkets of secret words, the music envelops,
Dancing around my body.
The sound, the feeling arresting me.*

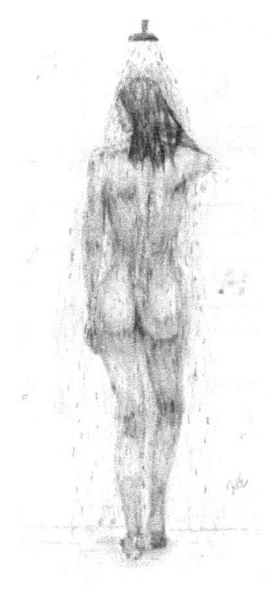

Liquid sound breathes joy into my body, lifting, giving
A warm breeze into my mouth,
blowing away the chill in me.

Deafened to the outside world,
I'm carried in your heart's ship.
Cocooned in a realm with no bordered,
yet alone together.

You engraved upon my heart, sweet murmurings.
The song too short.
In the ecstasy a memory, for now.

Awaiting the next song.

THOUGHTS

Thoughts of you
Are like flowers.

That float me on clouds
Severing the bonds

That forever
tie me to

The pains and misfortunes
Down here on earth.

SPEAKING

There's honesty in language of touch.
Your face against mine, a heart's window.
Your fingertips, a thousand words
Eyelashes blinking on my cheek
Stroke my soul like music.

Our bed-waltz is a dialogue.
Statement and response understood.
Lips against lips search deep
Where words have no place.
In the harmony of two notes.

The outside fills the inside
In perfect harbouring
Regardless of shape
Communicating more
Than mere narrative.

This conversation,
One beat to the next, speaks a truth
For a moment in time and space,
And a bond that contains
A promise of tomorrow.

COMIN' THRO THE RYE

*I speak for a time
when our bodies melded;
In nights under the stars and fireflies,
The days by the ocean,
the sun burning my bum;
In a cold stream,
our heat coursed through our veins.*

*I speak for the time
we fought over nothing worth bothering about;
Too tired to touch after busy days;
Fighting our kids into bed,
then dishes -
There was nothing left,
not even words.*

*I speak for the time
we clutched in despair
Trying to hang onto what was once there;
When your back was the only thing left;
When life's disappointments
 sucked us both dry.*

*I speak for the time
when our paths were changing
Our interests diverged
and threatened to crumble.*

*Where was the light
we'd ignited long ago?
One foot in front of the other,
alone like zombies
We struggled forward.*

*I speak for the time
when suddenly we saw
That life's ups and downs
were better shared.*

*I saw you anew
and appreciation returned,
Respect in your eyes
turned dark into light.*

*I speak for the time
when our souls re-melded;
The night under the covers
finding comfort anew;
Day doing chores
 without ego and rewards.*

*We still have the cold and the hot,
But together has more possibilties.*

THE INFINITE WALTZ

The notes rise to the sky.
It's an old harmony,
A shared song, known without being taught.

Two inhaling hearts,
Breathe another's breath,
Obliged to satisfy a universal desire.

The goat is looking for the doe,
A beaver builds a house for his mate,
A gibbon grooms its lover in the forest canopy,

The sand cranes dance together,
The bull moose knows the time of year.
The lady seahorse returns to her man to lay her eggs.

All creatures dance.
It's the same step by all in a waltz,
Seeking solace, fighting to mate

for immortality.

MADRIGAL OF FIRE

Teach me the fire
That passions my existence.
Teach me to respond
To infinite joys,
That ignites the fire.

Teach me to speak meaning
without words.
Teach me to awake
To the morning of life.

Teach me the notes
That resonate so sweetly.
Teach me the movements
Your body craves.

I long for a reason
To express my joy.
I long for a moment
To syncopate with you.

The duet of tomorrow
Beckons me to follow.
The waltz of companionship
Fills me with courage.

TOGETHER

We can walk together
On the beach
In the between life -
That space where dreams
collide with reality.
Witnessed by the sea and the sky,
Until I understand
That you love me.

SUNSHINE

Lover,
You are the sun that greets the morning
You are the rain that wills the plants to grow
You are the song that sings in my heart

My Love,
You have the power to summon me
from across the planet,
When I am down, you have the power
to bring the sun from
Behind the clouds and place it in my soul,
and in my heart.

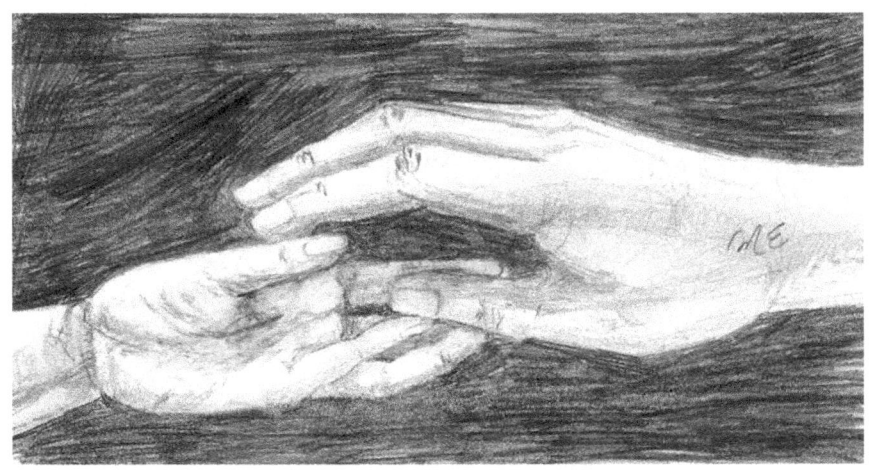

Friend,
I have energy to fly,
I have imagination to dream,
I have the will to climb tall mountains,

BECAUSE OF YOU.

END OF AN AFFAIRE

Your cheek sparking against my belly.
Fingertips contouring a thigh,
The inner sense flowing with the music,
Hearts gently undulating with the notes.

We rode the night horse,
And sailed with the sun ship,
Until, one morning, we woke to silence,
Sober-seeing what vanished without notice.

Last night? Last week?
Ten years slipped by so quickly
Gone is the sharp, articulate vision.
Living lonely now, with a memory.

What did we do?
What didn't we do?
Did we demand too much?
Or not enough?

These things resonate in my tissues, my bones.
These feelings now cast
indistinct shadows
on my present.

I ask :
Why did we
let go of each other?
Why did we
let go of the prize?

GLOOM INTO BRIGHTNESS

*I didn't know I lived
in black and white
until you gave me
your gift of colour.*

*When you fell in love with me,
I knew I would never get back.
When I fell in love with you,
I knew I would never want to return.*

*Your love gift.
Sent the darkness away.
Yesterday never existed
And today I see future.*

WE DANCED

My husband died yesterday.
Or maybe it was the day before.
My feet remember their movements
As we danced at our wedding.

My soul communicates with yours as we dance.

My wedding dress was lace.
I carried the primrose of spring.
I must get strawberries for your funeral.
You loved fresh fruit. But it's November.

My soul communicates with yours as we dance.

My tummy still has the weight I gained
while carrying Isobell. My clothes are tight.
What will you think?
The ugly duckling swimming so fast to keep up.

My soul communicates with yours as we dance.

Nicolas, now five, how can I answer you?
Your father will not read to you tonight.
But we are fine. We'll show them, OK?
You'll look well looked after - at the celebration.

My soul communicates with yours as we dance.

Your eyes meet mine in the dim of the moon.
You touch my face with fingertips, so gently.
In your heart a sacred inscription,
you asked me to read. "I love you."

My soul communicates with yours as we dance.

I still turn my head to you,
To tell you of some curios event.
My head rests on your pillow: "I love you,"
I communicate with you as I sleep.
You soul communicates with me as we dance.

"Gramma, I must drive you to the home,
It's almost time for dinner to be served."

THE PRIZE

I saw you standing in the doorway.
I didn't notice my breath.
What kind of apparition dares to intrude
Into my wonderful world?

My little boys, that I carry in my heart unit,
And the husband, I pledged to, are my team!
How dare you impose into my world
And take my breath away.

You evapourated like a mist
On a warm summer's day, because I asked,
But you stole something when you left.
How could you be so callous.

I resent your coming, and your going.
Why oh why did you come?
Give me back what you stole that day.
It wasn't at all kind.

Now that my precious teammate
has gone to ground,
here you are again,
asking to be a part of me.

I spent so long trying to erase you,
Cursing you each day.
I looked into the mirror everyday for years
only to see your soul looking back at me.

You say you love me.
How can that be true?
When you blotted
my contentment
for so long.

You say you left for my sake,
because I asked
But your intrusion
became my disease.

How can I love you now,
When you took my joy away?
When I've hated you so long,
How can I start to love you now?

There's no going back,
And no going forward.
We are stuck in a trespass,
Beyond our redemption.

MUSIC OF COMMUNION

*You are the one who has heard
the secrets in the notes I sing.
I am the listener of your notes
bubbling from deep in your being.
The song in the space between us,
is a fire that heats our home,
Cooks our food and entertains us
after the long day
working for our bread.*

THE BELLS OF SURRENDER

The speech of your body
took me from nowhere
to somewhere.
No longer lost
on a stormy sea,
My feet are located
On a solid shore.

My response
to your quest
brought such a delight,
expressed in your arms.
And what I felt on my lips
softly grounded my heart.

With lips upon lips.
and skin upon skin,
you locked me
within a capsule so close,
in tenderness mostly,
but also occasionally,
in an agony of passion.

*If words could be summoned,
the sky would have sung them.
Your request was surely more
than I could have thought possible.
So what could my heart do
but ring the bells of surrender.*

WHERE SELF-WORTH IS

For years I wondered steadfast asking,
Where does self-worth hide.

I looked for it in friends
I looked for it in family
I looked for it in degrees,
Awards, talents and luck.

I searched and searched.
Boy, did it hide itself well!
It was like
Looking for fish in the sky
And tigers in the Pacific.

I know what a
two-headed elephant looks like.
I knew I'd know it when I found it.
Clothes, cars, house, praise, stuff

Surly. I'd find it sooner or later

I saw others
Putting others down to appear higher,
Finding differences to seem superior,
Using guns, laws, rules, obedience, freedom.

I got older and older but still I searched.
Then some wisdom came my way.
I was looking in all the wrong places.
I was looking in the wrong direction.

Then some wisdom came my way.
A mirror was the place to start. Look inside.
A beginning, yes, but not easy or clear.
There was still a road to go, before I'm there

It was like standing in a station.
The train and destination
Blazoned On the board.
At last, I'm going the right way now.

Love responds to love
Respect to respect.
The train for sure will come,
And take me to my destination.

AFTER CREMATION

Gratitude -
For our time together,
that you will not have
this pain of separation,
And having learned what love is.

Pain -
For no more hugging,
no more planning a double future,
no longer playing together,
too much privacy,
no more us.

Anger -
For abandonment,
just the old single "me",
my loss,
doing everything myself.

Gratitude -
To have had a lover,
a protector,
a conspirator,
To have had a friend.

*But above all
to have had a friend
is priceless.
And that will
always be the case.
And you will come with me
Wherever I go.*

AFTER THE STORM

*I stand on the road
looking at the rubble
that was our house.
It had been difficult to find
without familiar landmarks.*

*Then my husband
puts his arm around my shoulders,
and our daughter
puts her arm in mine,
her husband
stands behind me,
with Jamie, safe in his arms,
who grabs my hair
And gurgles.*

*We are the lucky ones.
What more can the world offer?
We have everything.*

ENDURING

The touch of your fingers
and your kisses
on my skin
fills me with joy.

Though your fingers
and your lips
are no longer there,
their texture will always remain.

They didn't disappear
when you left,
because we had loved each other
with passion and truth,
and a spark that lit up the sky.

even though the love didn't last.

OPENING THE GATE

Our love is not only of the heart.
I love you with all of my senses,
My gestures, my waking, my sleeping,
walking, star-gazing, choosing,
The breath that I breathe.

*Now love has entered my world,
I cannot separate
one part of the universe from another.
In loving you, and being loved,
I now receive the love of the sun,
the trees, from the grasses
the wind that blows.*

*I cannot label this change in me,
It wasn't your love that created it.
Your love asked the question,
And my response awakened
a universe I didn't know was there.*

PASO DOBLE

Put your arms around me
I'll move my body with yours.
Hold my hand
And I'll come with you.
Kiss me gently
So I can taste your love.

I'll put my arms around you
So I can feel your body dance.
I'll hold your hand,
And we can arrive together.
I'll kiss you gently
So we can express our love.

www.ingramcontent.com/pod-product-compliance
Lightning Source LLC
Chambersburg PA
CBHW041319110526
44591CB00021B/2843